Japanese Celebrations

FOR CHILDREN

Festivals, Holidays and Traditions

by Betty Reynolds

TUTTLE Publishing

Tokyo | Rutland, Vermont | Singapore

O-Iwai Shimasho!

Let's Celebrate!

The people of Japan love to celebrate! There is a special day—whether it recognizes a change in the seasons, a religious observance, or just a special moment in life—in every month of the year. Ancient traditions, exotic decorations and delicious, seasonal foods come together to create wonderfully festive occasions.

Although Japan is a modern, fast-paced country, the Japanese people still honor their customs. They have celebrated their holidays and festivals in the same way for centuries. For example, many people still dress in their beautiful, traditional costume—the kimono—for special events.

Higasa ひがさ

A parasol leads the way in some Shinto ceremonies.

Hana-bi はなび

Fireworks are popular in summer.

Many of the holidays are based on Japanese religious beliefs. Today, the thousands of Buddhist temples and Shinto shrines serve as gathering places for families as they solemnly observe traditional religious rites, as well as joyfully eat, drink, shop and make merry. The shrine and temple grounds and the streets come alive—with strings of colorful paper lanterns overhead, and wall-to-wall with people shopping the street stalls.

The Japanese way of celebrating may seem very different to you, as it did to me when I lived in Tokyo. I hope this book takes you on an entertaining journey through a year of holiday fun in Japan.

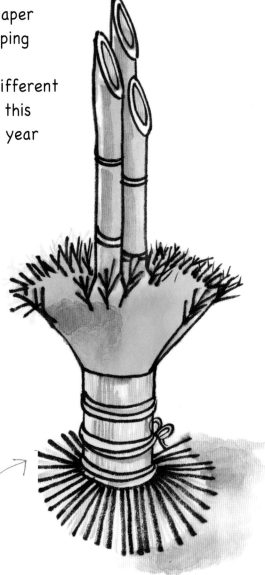

Kadomatsu かどまつ

Decorations made of pine straw and bamboo are placed in front of homes for the New Year celebration.

おしょうがつ

Ōshōgatsu

Japanese New Year

January 1st

Shortly before midnight on New Year's Eve, Buddhist priests appear carrying paper lanterns. Trickles at first, then streams, then rivers of people enter through the sacred gate and follow the priests into the temple. The smell of incense, the sounds of chanting and a large bell fill the air. All over Japan, families and friends are performing Hatsumōdé— the year's first worship at Buddhist temples and Shinto shrines to pray for good health and happiness. The New Year celebration is a joyous time that lasts several days. Special foods are prepared, debts are paid, houses are cleaned and decorations are hung to welcome back the Gods.

Hatsumōdé はつもうで

The first temple visit is a good time to pray for special favors in the year ahead. Here's how to pay respects to the Gods:

1 Purify your hands in the stone basin.

2 Pull the rope to ring the bell.

3 Make an offering, if you wish.

4 Bow twice.

5 Clap twice.

6 Bow once more.

Joya-no-Kané じょやのかね

People stand in line to ring out the 108 kinds of desire (who knew there were so many?) on New Year's Eve.

O-men おめん

Children love colorful masks of cartoon and folklore characters.

O-mikuji おみくじ

Determine your fortune by shaking a stick out of a box. Tie the written version on a tree.

After praying, people shop for symbols of good luck and protection.

Hamaya はまや

Evil-repelling arrows that can't poke out your eye.

だるま Daruma

Make a wish on the Paint in one black eye. When your wish comes true—paint in the other.

Ema えま

Write a vow or a special wish on a painted wooden tablet.

Dondo-yaki どんどやき

Last year's good luck tokens and decorations are burned in a bonfire as a way of thanking them for past performance.

おぞうに **O-Zóni:** A special soup containing O-mochi (pounded sticky-rice cakes). Chew carefully so you don't choke!

としこしそば
Toshi Koshi-soba:

Long noodles representing long life are eaten on New Year's Eve.

おせち りょうり **Osechi Ryóri:**

Foods representing health, happiness and a good harvest are prepared ahead and stored in a lacquer box.

Special foods are eaten during the New Year celebration.

もちつき
Mochitsuki:

くしだんご **Kushi-dango:** Rice dumplings grilled on a bamboo stick

Sticky-rice is pounded to make O-mochi on New Year's Eve.

やたい **Yatai**

Mobile street stalls sell other popular foods.

たいやき　おでん　たこ焼　お好み焼

たいやき
Tai-yaki:

A small cake filled with sweet beans represents happiness

おでん
Oden:

A stew of fish cake, tofu, egg and radish

たこやき
Tako-yaki:

Bits of octopus cooked in a batter

おこのみやき
Okonomi-yaki:

A pancake of seafood and vegetables cooked on a griddle

7

かるた
Karuta:

Traditional card games

たこあげ
Tako-agé

Kite-flying

↙ はねつき
Hané-tsuki:

Japanese
badminton

↑ はごいた
Hagoita

(Some people just collect
decorative paddles)

Other Traditional New Year's Pastimes

おとしだま
O-Toshidama

Children receive tiny
envelopes containing
generous gifts of money
from family members.

しちふくじん *Shichi-Fuku-jin:* The Seven Lucky Gods

↑だいこくてん ↑えびす   ↑べんざいてん ↑びしゃもんてん↖じゅろうじん と
Daikokuten Ebisu Benzaiten Bishamonten   ふくろくじゅ   *Hotei* ほてい
                                                      Jurōjin & Fukurokuju

The God   The   The Goddess   The God   The God of
of wealth   God of   of arts   of warriors   happiness
                 fishermen   The Gods of long life

ね
Ne: The rat is charming, honest and ambitious.

うし
Ushi: The ox is smart, reliable and sensible.

とら
Tora: Tigers are born leaders and competitive.

う
U: Rabbits are talented, sociable and well-spoken.

たつ
Tatsu: Dragons are elegant, healthy and strong.

み
Mi: The snake is beautiful, refined and subtle.

The year's zodiac animal becomes the symbol for the new year.

The zodiac "animal of the year" is often used on nenga-jō, (New Year's cards).

じゅうにし
Jūni-shi

The zodiac calendar follows a twelve-year cycle. Each year is named after one of the twelve animals. Many Japanese believe that you will have the same personality traits as the animal sign for the year you were born.

Which year were you born in? What animal represents that year? Do you match your animal sign?

Rat	1984	1996
Ox	1985	1997
Tiger	1986	1998
Rabbit	1987	1999
Dragon	1988	2000
Snake	1989	2001
Horse	1990	2002
Sheep	1991	2003
Monkey	1992	2004
Rooster	1993	2005
Dog	1994	2006
Boar	1995	2007

(Add or subtract 12 years to determine the year of each animal in the future or the past.)

うま
Uma: The horse is sporty, popular and a good team member.

ひつじ
Hitsuji: Sheep are creative, caring and trustful.

さる
Saru: The monkey is smart, impish and a crowd pleaser.

とり
Tori: Roosters are high-spirited, clever and artistic.

いぬ
Inu: The dog is active, honest and very loyal.

い
I: Boars are noble, fun-loving and industrious.

ゆき
Yuki
Snow

かまくら
Kamakura

A festival in northern Japan where children play in snow huts, honoring the God of water.

りきし
Rikishi
Wrestler

Hatsubasho はつばしょ

The first sumo tournament of the year starts on the second Sunday of January in Tokyo.

Other Celebrations in January

でぞめしき
Dezome-shiki

A 400-year-old tradition where firemen perform acrobatics high atop bamboo ladders propped up by poles held by other firemen.

いれずみ
Irezumi
Tattoo

せいじんの ひ *Seijin-no-hi*

Coming of Age Day—Second Monday of January

A national holiday when 20-year-olds are honored first in a civil ceremony and later at temples and shrines. They are officially adults and now have the right to vote.

はおり
Haori
Kimono jacket

ふりそで
Furisodé
Long-sleeved kimono

はかま
Hakama
Pleated skirt-like trousers.

わがし
Wa-gashi
Sweets made from beans and rice flour

まっちゃ
Matcha
Powdered green tea used in tea ceremonies.

うめまつり
Ume Matsuri

The Japanese people love nature. When the plum blossoms bloom in February—everyone takes notice.

うめ
Ume
Plum tree

Tea houses with plum trees nearby set up benches with parasols where they can serve green tea.

Setsubun

The Bean-Throwing Ceremony

February 3rd

According to the old lunar calendar of Japan, February 3rd marks the eve of the first day of spring. On that day, in an effort to ward off illness and misfortune, Japanese families scatter roasted soy beans inside their homes and out of every window and door. Someone, usually Dad, wears a mask representing a demon while the rest of the family pelts him with beans, shouting "Oni wa soto!" ("Out with the devil!"), "Fukuwa uchi!" ("In with good luck!"). In a wish for good luck, everyone eats one bean for every year of their age. This tradition is said to stem from the days when a demon terrorized townspeople at night. The ruling Emperor ordered seven wise men to throw beans in the demon's cave and seal up the exit.

まめ
Mamé

Beans

おに は そと！
"Oni wa soto!"
("Devil out!")

おに は そと！
"Oni wa soto!"
("Devil out!")

"Fuku wa uchi!"
("Good luck in!")
ふく は うち！

まめまき

Mamé-maki Bean throwing.
Ceremonies are also held at temples
and shrines where crowds try to catch
"lucky beans" tossed by celebrities.

Hina Matsuri
ひなまつり

The Doll Festival

March 3rd

On the 3rd day of March, families celebrate their pride in their daughters by displaying dolls of the Emperor and Empress in a prominent place in the home. Some doll sets also include all of the Imperial court attendants, musicians and possessions. These dolls are not played with. They are usually gifts from the grandparents or inherited from the girl's mother, and are quite delicate and expensive! They are unwrapped with ceremony, admired for a few weeks and then put back in their boxes. One popular superstition says if the dolls aren't returned to their boxes soon after the 3rd, the daughters will not get married.

ひなにんぎょう
Hina-ningyō

There are various types of hina dolls.
Some are made of paper.

Other Traditions Observed for Hina Matsuri

おちゃ
Ocha
Green tea

こんぺいとう
Kompeitō
Tiny sugar spheres

It's fun to dress in a kimono for the occasion.

さくらもち
Sakura-mochi
is wrapped in an edible cherry leaf.

しろざけ *Shiro-zaké*
A sweet saké made without alcohol

なまがし
Nama-gashi
Sweets made from sticky rice and sweet beans

はまぐり
Hamaguri
Clams cooked in broth are another must.

Gomokuzushi ごもくずし
and other sushi rice dishes are enjoyed during Hina Matsuri.

Children like to make hina dolls out of paper.
Here are two styles you can make!

1 Fold 3 small paper plates in half (one for the dolls' heads, one for each body).

2 Draw faces and kimono collars for the Emperor & Empress on the 1st plate.

3 Cut out the heads with scissors.

4 Cut off a corner of a colorful piece of paper for the Empress's kimono and glue on 2nd plate.

5 Attach the Empress's head to both sides of the plate with glue.

6 Repeat the process for the Emperor on the 3rd plate.
7 Glue on the Emperor's head.

A Start with a square piece of paper folded in half.

B Open back up & fold both corners into the center line.

C Now fold top corner down.

D Fold bottom half up as shown below.

E Fold in left side first.

F Overlap with the right side.

G Make 2 folds for the Emperor's hat.

H Fold back to make a base.

I Fold the point forward. for the Emperor. And backwards for the Empress

Everyone Loves Sakura!
さくら
Cherry Blossoms

All of Japan seems to catch spring fever when the cherry trees bloom. No one wants to be at school. They go out with friends picnicking, painting, photographing or just admiring the beauty of these short-lived blossoms. These parties are called Hanami. Most people are invited to several with different groups of friends or co-workers. Even tourists are invited to join in the fun. There are many famous places in Japan where there are so many cherry trees that you'll see a fairyland of pink overhead with a sea of people walking or sitting on blue tarps below. Enjoying lunchboxes and drinking rice wine called saké are important ingredients for the festivities. If you're lucky and the weather stays dry, the blossoms could last two whole weeks! But some years the rains wash them away in just a few days!

O-bentō おべんとう

People pack or buy a lunchbox filled with rice, vegetables and cooked and raw fish.

18

Sakura Zensen さくらぜんせん

"Cherry Blossom Front" forecasts are televised daily as the blooms move north from Okinawa to Hokkaido. The season runs from late March to mid-May.

Things to Do on a Hanami

ボート を こぐ
Bōto-wo-kogu

Row a boat

のる
Noru

Ride

おどる
Odoru

Dance!

うたう
Utau

Sing

たべる
Taberu

Eat

のむ
Nomu

Drink

けんぶつ する
Kenbutsu-suru

Watch others enjoy

Let's all go on a

はなみ

Hanami

Cherry Blossom Viewing Party

さくら　　さくら、　の　やま　も　さと　も
Sa-ku-ra,　　sa ku ra,　　No-ya-ma-mo sa-to-mo
On hills, in dales and villages, cherry blossoms

みわたす　　かぎ―り、　かすみ　か
Mi-wa-ta-su　　Ka-gi―ri,　　Ka-su-mi-Ka
cherry blossoms blooming everywhere

くも　か、　あさひ　に　にお―う
Ku-mo-ka,　　A-sa-hi-ni　　ni-ō ―
Like pink mists or clouds in morning light,

さくら　　さくら、　はな　ざ―かり
Sa-ku-ra　　Sa-ku-ra,　　ha-na-za―ka-ri
Cherry blossoms, cherry blossoms, glowing in full bloom

いぬ の さんぽ
Inu no sampo
Walk a dog

いぬ
Inu
Dog

ねる
Neru
Sleep

しゃしん を とる
Shashin wo toru
Take a photo

みる
Miru
Look

Kan-butsu-e
かんぶつえ

Buddha's Baptism Celebration

On the 8th of April Japan celebrates the birthday of Buddha, the founder of Buddhism—one of their major religions. Throughout Japan, miniature pavilions with a statue of the young Buddha are decorated with flowers and carried to Buddhist temples in colorful processions. Children who attend Buddhist study classes take turns pouring sweet tea over Buddha's head in a form of baptism. The statue then stays in place on the temple grounds for a few days so that others may pay their respects. This ceremony, also known as the Flower Festival, often occurs during the cherry blossom season.

はなまつり

はなみどう
Hanamidō

The "Flowery Temple" is delivered by a statue of an elephant wheeled into a famous temple in Tokyo.

こどものひ
Kodomo-no-hi
Children's Day
May 5th

For centuries Japan celebrated Boy's Day on the 5th day of the 5th month. In 1954 the festival became known as Kodomo-no-hi, a national holiday celebrating the healthy growth of all children—both boys and girls. Families with a son fly fish-shaped windsocks outside of their homes on a long pole. The windsocks, called Koi nobori, represent carp swimming upstream. Parents hope their sons will overcome obstacles as they grow up and become men. It is a treat to see all of the carp streamers flying high above the city and in the countryside. Kodomo-no-hi is part of Golden Week, a week of separate holidays when many families travel, visit amusement parks and just relax. Other holidays during that week include Greenery Day and Constitution Day.

こいのぼり
Koi nobori
Carp streamers

Other traditions for Children's Day include:

しょうぶ

Shōbu

A variety of iris whose long, pointed leaves are used in children's mock sword fights

かしわもち

Kashiwa-mochi

Rice-flour dumplings filled with a paste of sweet beans are wrapped in oak leaves.

ちまき

Chimak

Sweet rice dumplings wrapped in bamboo leaves are another favorite treat.

しょうぶゆ

Shōbu-yu

A hot bath scented with iris leaves enjoyed by fathers and sons

ごがつにんぎょう

Gogatsu-ningyō

Families with sons set up displays of samurai helmets and other martial symbols.

Here's how to make a samurai helmet from a piece of 2-toned origami paper:

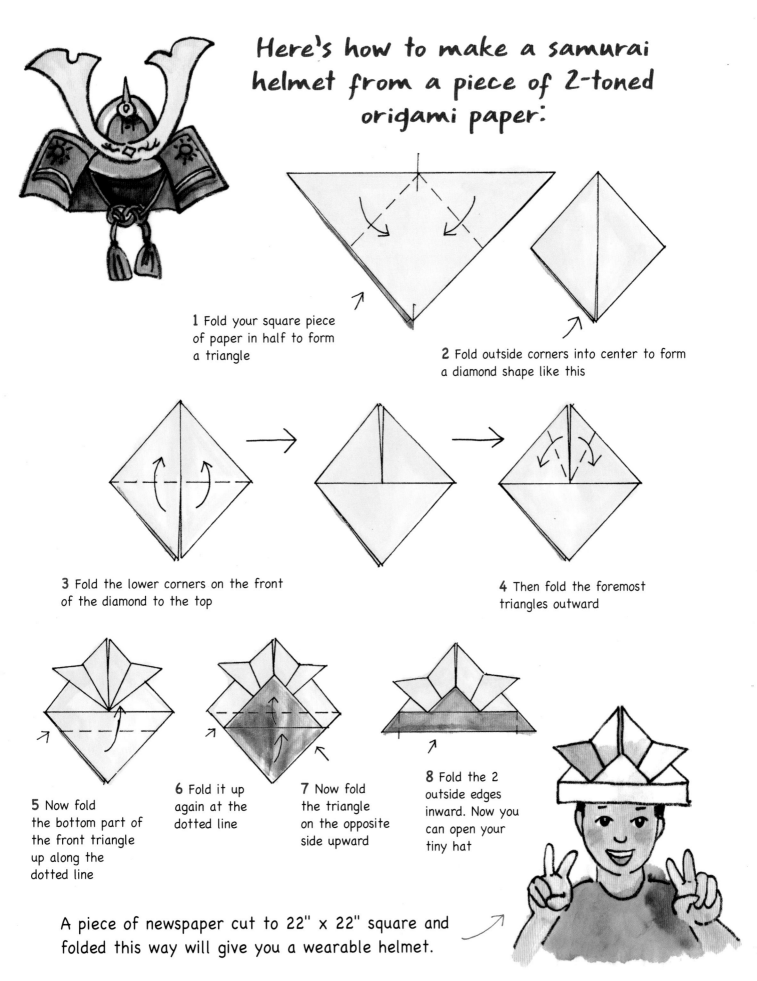

1 Fold your square piece of paper in half to form a triangle

2 Fold outside corners into center to form a diamond shape like this

3 Fold the lower corners on the front of the diamond to the top

4 Then fold the foremost triangles outward

5 Now fold the bottom part of the front triangle up along the dotted line

6 Fold it up again at the dotted line

7 Now fold the triangle on the opposite side upward

8 Fold the 2 outside edges inward. Now you can open your tiny hat

A piece of newspaper cut to 22" x 22" square and folded this way will give you a wearable helmet.

はなび
Hana-bi

Fireworks

うちわ
Uchiwa

Fan

ぞうり
Zōri

Thong
sandals

ゆかた
Yukata

A cotton kimono is often
worn to summer events.

なつ

Natsu

Summer

Although summers are very hot and humid
in Japan, there are plenty of things
to look forward to. School vacation,
sensational fireworks, public swimming
pools and numerous festivals and street
fairs distract children from the heat.

げた
Geta

Clogs

せんこう はなび
*Senkō
hana-bi*

Sparklers

28

てるてるぼうず
Teru-teru-bōzu

Rainy day boy. Rainy season, called tsuyu, lasts from mid-June to mid-July. Children make little dolls from tissues and hang them in a window to stop the dreary rain.

うなぎ
Unagi

Eel gives you stamina during the heat wave.

ふうりん
Fūrin

Glass wind chimes try to catch the slightest breeze.

そうめん
Sōmen

Cold noodles dipped in broth are very refreshing.

きんぎょすくい
Kingyo-sukui

Catching goldfish with a thin paper ladle is very tricky.

わたあめ
Wata-amé

Cotton candy

とうもろこし
Tōmorokoshi

Corn on the cob grilled with soy sauce

かきごおり
Kakigōri

Shaved ice with flavored syrup

やたい *Yatai:* Street stalls attract children of all ages during festival days.

Children often write about
the careers they would like
to have. This child would like
to become a doctor.

わたしは
しょうらい
おいしゃさんに
なりたいです

People in Sendai City celebrate
with huge ornaments of confetti
balls and streamers.

たなばた
Tanabata
The Star Festival
July 7th

According to an old legend, a king of the heavens separated his daughter, The Princess Weaver Star, from her husband, The Cow Herder Star, because their intense love kept them from their duties. Now they can only meet once a year—on the eve of July 7th—by crossing the Milky Way. If it rains, the star-crossed lovers will have to put off their reunion for another year. To celebrate this romantic story, people write poems and special wishes on colorful strips of paper called tanzaku, and hang them from the limbs of bamboo trees.

What would your
special wish be?
Write your own.

まつり

O-Bon

The Festival of Souls

August 13th–16th

O-Bon, a centuries-old Buddhist memorial festival, is a time to pay respects to one's ancestors. Families travel back to their hometowns for a 3-day reunion with their living relatives—and the spirits of the deceased. To welcome back the spirits, people pray at gravesites and in front of small altars in the family home. Often, a Buddhist priest is invited to say prayers. Although O-Bon is a solemn occasion, people enjoy spending time with their families. Lanterns are hung, and a tower for musicians is erected in a central location. Many people gather to perform a folk-dance called Bon-odori. Everyone is invited to join in. You don't need to be a good dancer to learn the steps. Just watch what the person in front of you is doing and follow them as they dance around in a big circle.

Lanterns are lit and tiny fires are set in front of homes to lead the spirits back.

A symbolic meal is placed on a small altar for the spirits of the dead.

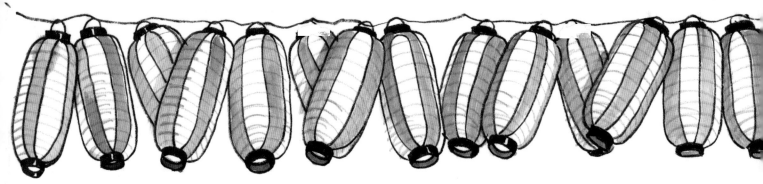

Matsuri
まつり

Festivals

Throughout the centuries, summer festivals
were held to ward off floods and epidemics. Fall
festivals were dedicated to good harvests. Most
areas in Japan host a special matsuri during these
seasons. In some celebrations, parades of people
carry portable Shinto shrines called mikoshi
through the streets. Chanting "wa shoi, wa shoi!"
the bearers start and stop, move forward and
get pushed backwards, giving the shrine's spirits
a very rowdy ride. Hopefully, the Gods will feel
properly thanked for the past harvests and
continue to provide good ones for years to come.

Hanten はんてん
Short festival coat

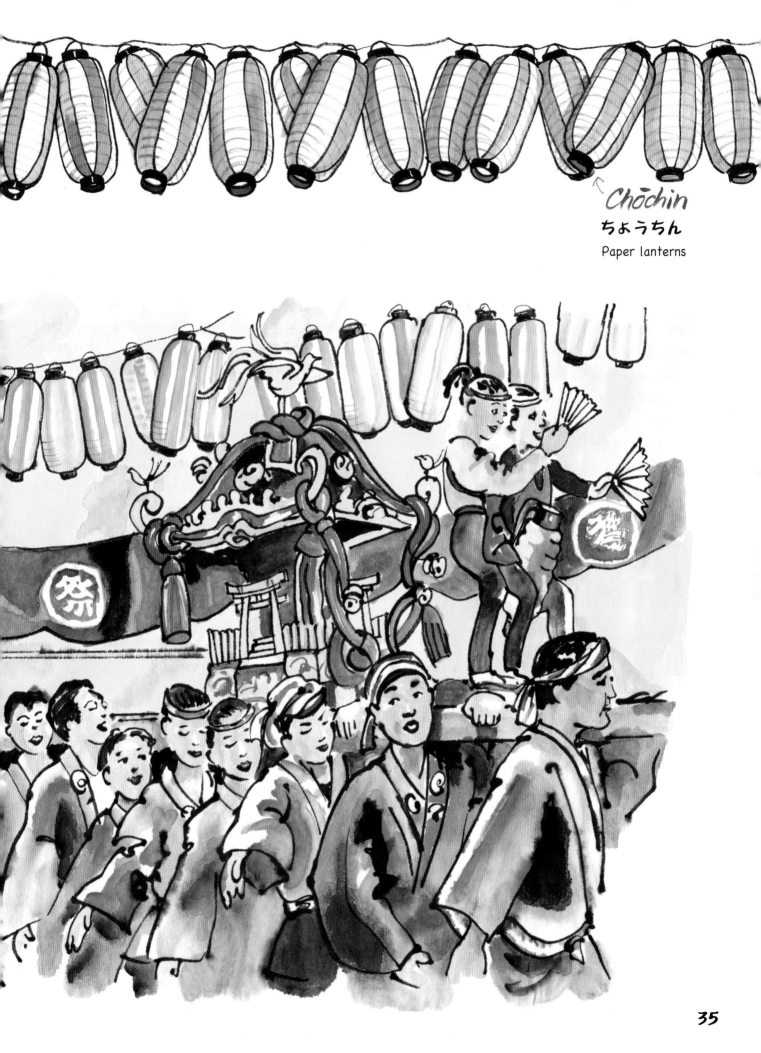

Chōchin
ちょうちん
Paper lanterns

Children often participate in a matsuri.

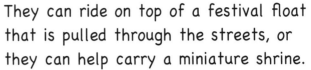

They can ride on top of a festival float that is pulled through the streets, or they can help carry a miniature shrine.

They can perform in a traditional drum troupe (which requires hard practice).

At one festival in Tokyo, children throw pails of water at each other to keep everyone cooled down.

あわ おどり
Awa Odori
Thousands participate in this folk dance on the island of Shikoku.

そうま のまおい
Sōma Nomaoi
A fantastic pageant where hundreds of riders on horseback fight for a battle flag in Soma City

Many regions in Japan have their own special matsuri. Here are just three examples.

ねぶた
Nebuta
A festival dedicated to the God of sleep has illuminated floats and many energetic dancers in Aomori City.

うんどうかい
Undo-Kai

Athletic Meets

September through October

You can usually hear these competitions before you see them. You'll hear roars from the crowd, cheers from the winners and groans from the losers. Meets are often held on weekends so parents can attend. Two teams compete in foot races and traditional games.

Tama-iré たまいれ

Two teams compete to see who gets the most balls in a basket.

Jan-Ken じゃんけん

Japanese children have their own version of the traditional game rock, paper, scissors. Here's how to play: Two players form their hands into the shape of a stone, a paper or scissors while shouting "Jan-ken-pon!" The player with two wins out of three goes first in the competition.

Winner	Loser		Winner	Loser		Winner	Loser

  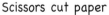 

Stone smashes scissors   Scissors cut paper   Paper covers stone

つなひき
Tsuna-hiki

Tug of war

おつきみ
O-Tsukimi
Moon Viewing
September

つき
Tsuki
Moon

September's beautiful full moon invites admiration and inspires people to write haiku (poems). Small altars with traditional decorations are set up in prime viewing areas in homes.

In some parts of the world people see "the man in the moon" in the craters and seas. The Japanese see a rabbit pounding rice cakes! Can you see him from your country?

The moon—how big and round and red and bright! Children, to whom does it belong tonight?

—A translation of a famous moon-viewing haiku by Issa

39

しちごさん
Shichi-gosan
7-5-3 Festival

November 15th

On November 15th girls aged seven and three, and boys aged five and three, are taken to their local shrine to be presented to the Gods. Their parents offer thanks and pray for their continued happiness and health. Some children wear their best modern clothes, but children dressed in traditional kimono and sandals attract most of the attention.

祝七五三

ちとせあめ
Chitosé-amé

"Thousand-year" candy is eaten to celebrate the event.

Hordes of local people, tourists and TV cameramen visit Meiji Shrine in Tokyo on the Sundays before and after the 15th to take photographs. Children don't seem to notice their celebrity. They are far more interested in the bags of candy they receive.

Sono-ta no-Gyôji

Other Happy Events

おみやまいり
O-Miyamairi

Baby's First Visit to a Shrine

When a boy is 32 days old, and a girl
is 33 days old, his or her grandmother
takes the child to a local Shinto shrine
to be presented to the Gods. A Shinto
priest waves a wand of sacred paper
over the baby's head to drive away
evil spirits and to pray for blessings
and protection. There is usually a
celebration afterwards.

いぬはりこ
Inu-hariko →

Papier-mache dogs are given
to the baby symbolizing
growth and vitality.

Gohei ごへい

A paper wand symbolizing the purifying nature of fire

おくいぞめ
O-Kuizomé

Baby's First Meal

This tradition usually takes place on the 100th day after birth. The family gathers at a restaurant, and the baby is presented with a ceremonial meal. With chopsticks, a parent places a grain of rice into the baby's mouth. Then the rest of the family has a great time eating and drinking.

たんじょうび
Tanjō-bi

Birthday

A special birthday meal includes rice cooked with red beans. It is followed by cake and presents.

さんさんくど
San-san-kudo

The groom and then the bride take three sips of sacred wine from each of the three cups. Then they pledge to stay together.

けっこんしき
Kekkon-shiki
Weddings

Japanese Shinto weddings combine the traditional with the modern. The bride and groom walk in a grand procession across the shrine grounds accompanied by attendants, parents, family and friends. After a Shinto priest performs a purification ceremony, the couple drinks rice wine and exchanges vows and wedding rings. Then the whole party gathers for a group photograph. At the reception afterwards, held at a chic restaurant, the bride will change out of her kimono into a white wedding gown and the groom will put on a tuxedo.

しゅうぎぶくろ

Shūgi-bukuro

Guests give gifts of money in special envelopes.

たい の おかしらつき
Tai-no-okashiratsuki

A ceremonial fish called tai
(seabream) is served to signify
the happiness of the union.

Japanese Words Used in This Book

Japanese children first learn to write in basic symbols called hiragana. Each symbol is a separate syllable that has its own unique sound. When these symbols are combined they form Japanese words. Here are clues to help you pronounce some words in this book:

おしょうがつ	O-Shōgatsu (Oh-show-gah-tsue)
はつもうで	Hatsumōdé (Hah-tsue-mowdey)
せつぶん	Setsubun (Sey-tsue-boon)
ひなまつり	Hina Matsuri (Hee-nah-mahtsue-ree)
さくら	Sakura (Sah-koo-rah)
はなみ	Hanami (Hah-nah-mee)
かんぶつえ	Kan-butsu-e (Kahn-bootsue-eh)
こども の ひ	Kodomo-no-hi (Koh-doh-moh-no-hee)
なつ	Natsu (Nah-tsue)
たなばた	Tanabata (Tah-nah-bah-tah)
おぼん	O-Bon (Oh-Bohn)
まつり	Matsuri (Mah-tsue-ree)
うんどうかい	Undō-kai (Uhn-doh-kigh)
おつきみ	O-Tsukimi (Oh-tsue-kee-mee)
しちごさん	Shichi-go-san (Shee-chee-go-sahn)
おみやまいり	O-Miyamairi (Oh-Mee-yah-mah-ree)
おくいぞめ	O-Kuizomé (Oh-Kooee-zoh-mee)
たんじょうび	Tanjō-bi (Tan-joe-bee)
けっこんしき	Kekkon-shiki (Keh-kon-she-kee)

46

VOWELS

		A (ah)	I (ee)	U (oo)	E (eh)	O (oh)
sounds like						
		あ a	い i	う u	え e	お o
CONSONANTS	K	か ka	き ki	く ku	け ke	こ ko
	S	さ sa	し shi	す su	せ se	そ so
	T	た ta	ち chi	つ tsu	て te	と to
	N	な na	に ni	ぬ nu	ね ne	の no
	H	は ha	ひ hi	ふ fu	へ he	ほ ho
	M	ま ma	み mi	む mu	め me	も mo
	Y	や ya		ゆ yu		よ yo
	R	ら ra	り ri	る ru	れ re	ろ ro
	W	わ wa				を wo
ん	N					

In memory of Elizabeth Reynolds and Vera Maher who turned every family gathering into a celebration

かがみもち
Kagami-mochi

An offering to the Gods
made of pounded rice

どうも ありがとう
Dōmo Arigatō "Thank You"

Thank you to my many friends in Japan who so generously shared their culture and their holidays. And a special thanks to my editor, Ed Walters.

Published by Tuttle Publishing, an imprint of Periplus Editions (HK) Ltd.

www.tuttlepublishing.com

LCC Card No. 2005934420

ISBN 978-4-8053-1738-9

Distributed by:

North America, Latin America & Europe
Tuttle Publishing
364 Innovation Drive
North Clarendon, VT 05759-9436 U.S.A.
Tel: 1 (802) 773-8930
Fax: 1 (802) 773-6993
info@tuttlepublishing.com
www.tuttlepublishing.com

Japan
Tuttle Publishing
Yaekari Building, 3rd Floor 5-4-12
Osaki Shinagawa-ku,
Tokyo 141 0032
Tel: (81) 3 5437-0171
Fax: (81) 3 5437-0755
sales@tuttle.co.jp
www.tuttle.co.jp

Asia Pacific
Berkeley Books Pte. Ltd.
3 Kallang Sector #04-01
Singapore 349278
Tel: (65) 6741 2178
Fax: (65) 6741 2179
inquiries@periplus.com.sg
www.tuttlepublishing.com

26 25 24 23
10 9 8 7 6 5 4 3 2 1

Printed in China
2211EP

"Books to Span the East and West"

Tuttle Publishing was founded in 1832 in the small New England town of Rutland, Vermont [USA]. Our core values remain as strong today as they were then—to publish best-in-class books which bring people together one page at a time. In 1948, we established a publishing outpost in Japan—and Tuttle is now a leader in publishing English-language books about the arts, languages and cultures of Asia. The world has become a much smaller place today and Asia's economic and cultural influence has grown. Yet the need for meaningful dialogue and information about this diverse region has never been greater. Over the past seven decades, Tuttle has published thousands of books on subjects ranging from martial arts and paper crafts to language learning and literature—and our talented authors, illustrators, designers and photographers have won many prestigious awards. We welcome you to explore the wealth of information available on Asia at **www.tuttlepublishing.com**.